Robin Hood

AND HIS MERRY MEN

A classic story adapted by Gill Munton

Series Editor: Louis Fidge

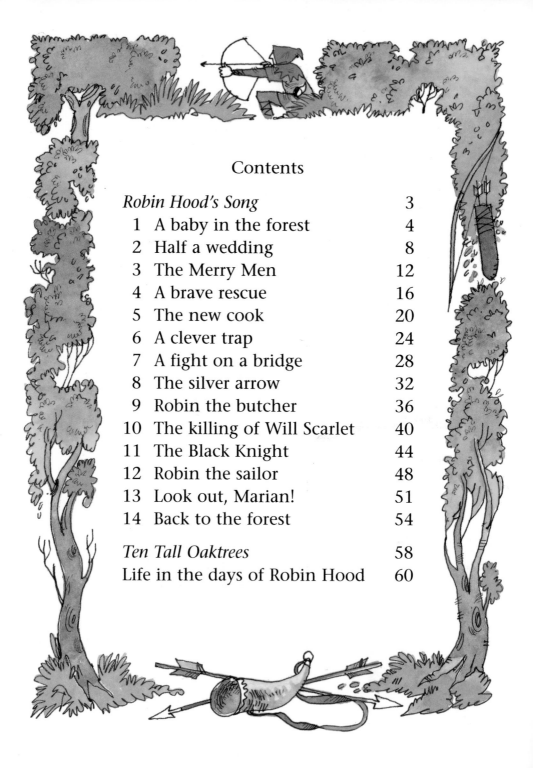

Contents

ROBIN HOOD'S SONG

Robin Hood, Robin Hood, riding through the glen,
Robin Hood, Robin Hood, with his band of men,
Feared by the bad,
Loved by the good,
Robin Hood, Robin Hood, Robin Hood.

King Richard is away at war. His brother, bad Prince John,
is ruling England. He makes the people pay lots of taxes.
When they cannot pay, he takes their houses and their land.

CHAPTER 1
A baby in the forest

Sir Robert of Locksley and his wife Joanna lived in Sherwood Forest with their baby, Robin.

They were hiding from Joanna's father. He did not like Sir Robert, and had threatened to kill him. So after their wedding, they left Sir Robert's home at Locksley Hall, near Nottingham, and went to live in the Forest.

Robin was born there, on a bed of green leaves.

One day, as Joanna sat under a tree with her baby in her arms, a bearded man on a white horse came crashing through the forest. Sir Robert picked up his sword.

'So *this* is where you are hiding!' said the man. He jumped down from his horse.

'Father!' said Joanna. She held Robin tightly in her arms.

'And this is baby Robin, hmm?' said Joanna's father. 'The baby who will be Sir Robin of Locksley one day? Well, well! He's a handsome boy. He has your black eyes.'

'What do you want?' asked Sir Robert.

'When you took my daughter away from me, I wanted to punish you,' said Joanna's father. 'But that was two years ago. I think I am a better man now. And Robin is my first grandson. I want to forgive you – and I want us to be friends. What do you say?'

Joanna laughed, and put Robin in her father's arms.

'I say – that is what *we* want, too, Father!' she said.

Sir Robert put down his sword and shook hands with Joanna's father.

Then Sir Robert, his wife and little Robin left the forest, and went back to live at Locksley Hall.

When Robin was ten, he heard his father talking about the Sheriff of Nottingham.

'The Sheriff always wants more taxes, Joanna! We have no money, but we *must* pay. The Sheriff is the best of friends with Prince John – and Prince John thinks he is the King!'

Robin was fifteen on the day the Sheriff's men came and took his father away.

'My name is Sir Guy of Gisborn,' said one of the men. 'I am here to do the Sheriff's work. You did not pay all your taxes, Sir Robert, so now you must go to prison!'

Sir Guy's men tied Sir Robert's hands and feet together, and threw him on a horse. Then they galloped away.

Robin and his mother never saw Sir Robert again. But they often thought of him.

One day, when they were eating their dinner, Robin said, 'The people in Sherwood Forest are hungry, Mother. Prince John says they cannot kill the deer, but the people have no money and there is no other food. I am going to help those people, Mother.'

CHAPTER 2
Half a wedding

Five years later, Prince John and the Sheriff of Nottingham were eating dinner together.

'Married? Robin of Locksley is getting married?' said Prince John. He stroked his black beard, lost in thought. 'That young man is as bad as his father. He hunts deer, and tells people not to pay my taxes!'

'He *thinks* he is getting married,' said the Sheriff of Nottingham. He ate another mouthful of meat. 'But instead, he is going to prison! This is a good time to capture him. The wedding is tomorrow, but the wedding dinner is tonight at Locksley Hall. Let's go to the dinner. We can wear the clothes of forest people so that no one recognises us. Let's see what we can find out.'

That night, Prince John and the Sheriff of Nottingham went to Locksley Hall. They ate a good dinner, but they watched and listened, too.

They saw Robin and his bride, Marian, with their families and friends. They were happy and laughing. And they heard a boy, no more than twelve years old, telling Robin his story.

'My name is Much – I am the miller's son. Ten of the Sheriff's men came to our mill with swords! My father was working in the mill. They didn't give him a chance – they told him that his flour was too expensive, and then they threw a burning branch and set fire to the mill ...'

Much started to cry, and Robin put his arm round him.

He said, 'The Sheriff is a bad man. Now you have no father, Marian and I will help you all we can. But England will not be a happy place until King Richard is home, and Prince John has gone.'

The two spies had heard all they needed to hear.

Robin of Locksley must die!

Robin smiled at Marian. She looked beautiful in the morning light that came in through the long window.

'I love you with all my heart,' he said.

The abbot opened his mouth to say the words that would make them man and wife.

But then the big wooden door crashed open, and a man walked in. He held a long, sharp sword above his head.

'Stop!' he shouted. 'I am here to do the work of the Sheriff of Nottingham. This wedding cannot continue!'

The abbot said, 'You are Sir Guy of Gisborn, I think. This wedding is not against the law of the land. Why do you come here with your sword in your hand, and say that it cannot continue?'

'This man is Robin of Locksley!' cried Sir Guy. 'He hunts the deer in the forest, and makes trouble for the Sheriff and our good Prince John. I am going to take him to Nottingham, where he will be punished!'

'Sir Guy,' said Robin. 'You have come here with a sword. As you can see, it is my wedding day – so *I* do not have one! But I am happy to fight you!'

And he ran towards Sir Guy with his fists raised.

The fight did not last long. Sir Guy and his men could not beat Robin and his friends, and they soon ran away.

When the fight was over, Robin said, 'Marian – your father will look after you until we can be together again.'

Then he spoke to his best friend, Will Scarlet.

'Come, Will! We'll hide in Sherwood Forest, where we will make trouble for the Sheriff – and lots of it!'

Robin and Will Scarlet jumped on their horses and galloped off towards the forest.

CHAPTER 3
The Merry Men

Robin was making arrows with his knife. He sang a song as he worked.

'Robin! What do you think of this?'

Robin stopped singing and put down his knife. He looked up. Will Scarlet was sitting on a log, smiling at him. Will was sewing some clothes with a needle and thread. He held up a green jacket with a hood.

'Do you like it? I could make one for you,' he said.

'Keep sewing, Will, and make jackets for us all!' said Robin. 'We must all wear green clothes. Then no one can see us in the forest. We will all look the same, and we will be called … the Merry Men! I will be called Robin Hood!

That night, Robin and the Merry Men sat round the fire together.

'I have a plan,' said Robin. 'We will take money from rich people, and give it to poor people. We will not take all their money – we will only take half. And we will try not to hurt anyone. The best place to take the money is in the forest. Many people ride through it on their way to Nottingham. We will stop them, give them a good dinner in our camp – and then we will ask them to pay for it!'

The Merry Men laughed. It was going to be fun in the forest!

The Sheriff of Nottingham soon heard about the Merry Men. He was worried – more men joined Robin every day. Many others who lived in the forest were Robin's friends.

One day, Will Scarlet and Much were fishing in the river when they saw smoke rising above the trees.

'They're fighting us with fire!' Will cried. 'Let's go and tell Robin.'

They took their fish, and started to walk back to the camp.

'Stop! Who goes there?'

Will looked up in surprise. A boy in a blue jacket and a red hood stood on the path. He held a long sword.

'Has the Sheriff sent you?' asked Will. 'You are just a boy! I will not be your prisoner – you will be mine!'

He grabbed the boy and tied his hands behind his back.

When they arrived at the camp, Will pushed the boy towards Robin.

'This boy is from the Sheriff of Nottingham,' he told Robin. 'He wanted to take us prisoner.'

The boy looked at Robin and pulled down his hood. Long golden hair fell onto his shoulders and down his back.

'Marian!' cried Robin. 'We all thought you were a boy!'

'I've come to join the Merry Men!' said Marian.

'I'm so happy to see you!' Robin cried. 'But living in the forest is dangerous.'

'I want to be with you all,' said Marian. 'And there's another thing – I think my father wants me to marry Sir Guy of Gisborn, because he's rich.'

'I will never let you marry that man!' cried Robin. 'Do you have any news of my home, Locksley Hall?'

'The news is bad, Robin,' said Marian. 'People say that Sir Guy lives there now!'

'Sir Guy of Gisborn lives in *my* house?' gasped Robin. 'Will – take Much to Locksley, and find out if this is true!'

CHAPTER 4
A brave rescue

Much took a deep breath.

'We did as you said, Robin. We went to Locksley Hall. But when we were in the garden, Will told me to stay outside and hide in the bushes. He didn't want me to be in danger.

'Will climbed into the Hall through a window. I waited in the bushes for a long time, but he didn't come out. Then suddenly, the door opened and Sir Guy pushed Will out. Will's hands were tied behind his back.

'Sir Guy started to shout at Will. He said, "I know who you are! You're a friend of Robin Hood, and he sent you here to spy on me! Well, I'll tell you what I do with spies – I hang them! I'm taking you to the prison in Nottingham. And at midday tomorrow – you will hang!"

'And then Sir Guy's men took Will away! There was nothing I could do to help him, Robin ...'

Much started to cry.

'But you *have* helped him,' said Robin. 'You have found out where he is. And now I must go and rescue him!'

The next morning, Robin put on a long cloak over his green clothes, and set off for Nottingham. First, he went to the hangman's house.

'The Sheriff has sent me,' he said, when the hangman opened the door. 'Will you let me in?'

The hangman yawned and rubbed his eyes.

'Are you tired?' Robin asked. 'Then my news will make you happy. The Sheriff says that there will be no hangings today. You can have a holiday! Now – go back to bed.'

As he walked to the town square, Robin laughed at the way he had fooled the hangman.

But he stopped laughing when he saw his friend Will Scarlet. Will stood on a scaffold with a rope around his neck. The Sheriff was there. He was talking to Sir Guy of Gisborn. A crowd of town people stood and watched.

Robin quickly pulled his hood down over his face and walked up to the Sheriff.

'I think you are waiting for the hangman, sir,' he said. 'I have come to tell you that he is not well, and I am here to do his work. Is this Will Scarlet? Let's hang him now!'

Robin climbed up onto the scaffold and said something to Will. As he did so, he untied the ropes round Will's hands and neck, and pulled a sword from beneath his cloak. He handed it to Will. Then he pulled out his bow and arrow, and turned to face the Sheriff.

'I, Robin Hood, am the "hangman"!' Robin cried, and he shot an arrow into the air above the Sheriff's head. 'I am not here to hang Will Scarlet – I am here to rescue him!'

The Sheriff's mouth opened in surprise. As quick as a flash, Robin and Will jumped on two horses and galloped away from the town square. Soon they were safe in Sherwood Forest.

19

CHAPTER 5

The new cook

One day, Robin was walking by the river. He was looking for deer. The forest trees shaded him from the hot sun. He smiled as he thought about the way he had rescued Will.

Then he saw a little boat. A very fat man was untying it from a tree.

'Good morning, sir!' cried the man when he saw Robin. 'Do you want to cross the river?'

Robin thought about this. He did not want to cross the river, but he thought he would have some fun.

'Yes, please,' he said, and he climbed into the boat.

As he rowed across the river, the fat man told his story.

'My name is Friar Tuck. I had to leave my abbey because I spoke against the Sheriff of Nottingham. Now I row people across the river for a living.'

When they reached the other side of the river, the fat man said, 'Let me help you out of the boat, sir. Now, you must pay me two gold coins.'

Robin said, 'I think I want to cross the river again – please take me back to the other side.'

'Back to the other side?' said Friar Tuck, surprised.

But he did as Robin asked.

'Now, sir,' he said, 'you must pay me *four* gold coins.'

'I have no gold,' said Robin. 'I will pay you in another way. Climb onto my back, and *I* will take *you* across the river.'

'He is having fun with me,' said Friar Tuck to himself. 'A little fun never hurt anyone.'

He climbed onto Robin's back, and they set off across the river. When they reached the middle, Robin stood up straight. Friar Tuck fell into the water.

'You scoundrel!' cried Friar Tuck as he spat out a mouthful of river water.

'I am no scoundrel,' cried Robin, raising his fists. 'I am Robin Hood!'

But they did not fight. Instead, they started to laugh.

'Will you be one of my Merry Men?' said Robin. 'You are a good boatman – and I think you will be a brave fighter.'

'I am a good cook, too! And I am greedy,' laughed Friar Tuck. 'That's why I am so fat! Would you like me to cook for you and the other Merry Men?'

'I would like that very much!' said Robin. 'Come back to our camp, and you can cook your first dinner for Robin Hood!'

It was a good dinner. When they had all finished eating, the Merry Men sat round the fire, talking and laughing.

Suddenly, Robin jumped to his feet.

'Friar Tuck!' he said. 'You have cooked a good dinner for us. Now there is one more thing I would like you to do.'

'Name it, and I will do it.'

'Marian and I have only had half a wedding,' said Robin. 'We have Sir Guy of Gisborn to thank for that. You are a friar – will you finish our wedding for us?'

'I would like that very much!' smiled Friar Tuck.

CHAPTER 6

A clever trap

Robin heard a horse gallop up and stop outside his tent. 'Robin! Robin Hood! It's your old friend, Sir Richard of Leigh!'

Robin came out of his tent.

'Richard! It's good to see you,' he said. 'Come in, and tell me your news.'

Sir Richard of Leigh jumped off his horse, and followed Robin into the tent.

'Friar Tuck has just made some bread. Would you like some?' asked Robin.

'Yes, please,' said Sir Richard. 'I have not eaten today. I have no money for food. The Sheriff has taken it all. His men are taking my money to Nottingham right now.'

Robin looked at his friend.

'Don't worry. I will get your money back for you,' he told him. 'But we must hurry.'

Robin blew on his horn, to call the Merry Men.

'Now listen,' said Robin. 'The Sheriff's men are riding through the forest with Sir Richard's money! But I have a plan. First, I want you all to dig a big hole, a little way from the path. Cover it with branches and leaves, and then go and hide in the trees.'

'What are *you* going to do, Robin?' one of them asked.

'I am going to take my bow and arrow, and go to hunt deer,' he replied.

The Merry Men were surprised by this, but they did not ask any more questions. They went to dig the hole.

Robin waited under a tree with his bow and arrow. He pretended to hunt deer, but he was listening for the sound of horses.

Soon he heard horses' hooves on the path. Then he heard a voice.

'Sheriff! Look at that man with the bow and arrow. I think it's Robin Hood!'

'That scoundrel! He's hunting deer – right under my nose! Ha! But he hasn't seen us. This is my chance to make him my prisoner!'

The Sheriff turned his horse away from the path, and his men followed. They all galloped towards Robin. They shouted and waved their swords.

Then they reached the trap! One after another, the horses stumbled and fell through the branches and leaves that covered the hole. The men fell off their horses and tumbled in, too. Some of the horses jumped out, and galloped away.

Robin laughed, and blew his horn. The Merry Men ran from their hiding places and crowded round the trap.

The Sheriff and his men lay at the bottom of the hole. Robin and his Merry Men jumped in and took their swords away.

Then the Sheriff's horse jumped out of the hole, and Robin heard the jingle of coins in its saddlebags. He untied the saddlebags, and waved goodbye to the Sheriff as he carried them off into the forest.

Back at the camp, Robin opened the fat saddlebags and tipped out the gold coins.

'Look at this!' he cried. 'Sir Richard's money is all here – and there is more!' Robin smiled. 'That will be our pay, for all our hard work!'

CHAPTER 7

A fight on a bridge

A few weeks later, Robin was walking beside the river, with his bow under his arm, when he came to a bridge. He knew there were deer on the other side of the river, and he started to cross.

But there was another man on the bridge – a tall man with wide shoulders. He was coming the other way, and there was not room for them to pass each other.

Robin waved and called out to the man.

'Good morning! I want to cross the bridge – will you go back to the other bank, please? When I have crossed, it will be your turn.'

But the man did not move.

'No, I will not,' he said. 'Why must you cross first?'

'Because I am Robin Hood!' cried Robin. He fitted an arrow to his bow and pointed it at the man.

'Wait!' said the man. 'You have a bow and arrow, but I have only a stick. If we are going to fight, it must be a fair fight.'

'Very well,' said Robin. He found a long stick, and put down his bow and arrow.

'My name is John Little,' said the man. 'And I can beat *you* in a fight, any day!'

He raised his arm, and brought his stick down on Robin's back with a thump.

'You scoundrel!' cried Robin. 'I will show you who is the better fighter!'

This made John Little angry, and he pushed Robin in the chest. Robin stumbled and fell into the river.

Splash!

Robin was completely soaked. He stood up and stared at John Little. John Little stared back at Robin. Then the two men started to laugh.

John Little held out his hand to Robin, and helped him out of the river.

'Your clothes will soon dry,' he said. 'The sun is hot today.'

Robin tipped the water out of his horn. Then he blew it, to call his Merry Men.

When they arrived, Robin said, 'This man pushed me into the river!'

He smiled.

'Then I will do the same thing to him!' cried Will Scarlet, raising his fists.

'No,' said Robin. 'I don't want such a strong man to be my enemy. I want him to be my friend! John Little, will you be one of my Merry Men? You can show us how to fight!'

'I have heard that the Sheriff of Nottingham is your enemy,' said John Little. 'And he is mine, too! Yes, I will join the Merry Men!'

'Good!' laughed Robin. 'But first I want to change your name. Because you are so tall and wide, I will call you – Little John!'

Everyone laughed. Then Robin and his men led their new friend back to the camp.

CHAPTER 8
The silver arrow

'Robin! Have you heard the news?' cried Much. 'There is going to be an archery competition!'

Much had just come back from Nottingham, where he had visited his older sister.

Robin knew that the Sheriff was very angry with him. It would be dangerous to go to Nottingham and take part in the archery competition.

'My sister says that the prize will be a silver arrow! The Sheriff will give the prize to the winner!' Much added.

Robin thought about the silver arrow, and the Sheriff.

'I *will* do it!' he said.

On the day of the competition, Robin said goodbye to Marian and went to Nottingham with Will Scarlet.

In the town square, he saw a crowd of people. They were waiting for the competition to start. On one side of the square there was a target, with rings of white, black, blue, red and, in the middle, gold. The archers stood and talked to each other, and checked their arrows. The Sheriff and Sir Guy of Gisborn were there. Robin was surprised to see Prince John as well!

'I can have some fun today,' Robin said to himself.

It was September, and the sun was strong. All the archers had their hoods up to shade their eyes. Robin smiled to himself as he pulled up his own hood.

'My hood will shade my eyes,' he thought, 'but it will hide my face, too! No one will know that I am Robin Hood!'

The competition began. By noon, there were two archers left – the two with the highest scores. One of them was Robin.

'You two!' said the Sheriff. 'You can have three arrows each – the one with the higher score will be the winner!'

Each man fired his first arrow.

'Gold – for both of you!' cried the Sheriff as he pulled the arrows out of the gold ring in the middle of the target.

Each man fired his second arrow.

'Gold, again!' the Sheriff cried.

The other man raised his bow, and fired his last arrow. The crowd gasped.

'It's in the red ring!'

Now it was Robin's turn. Could he do it? He raised his arm and pulled back his last arrow. He fired.

'Gold!' cried the Sheriff. 'Well done, young man! Come and get your prize!'

Robin held out his hand for the silver arrow.

But the Sheriff said, 'Pull back your hood! We all want to see the winner's face!'

Robin had to pull back his hood.

'It's Robin Hood!' cried a voice in the crowd. 'He's the best archer in England!'

'So, Robin Hood,' said the Sheriff quietly. 'You are my prisoner at last! Now you will die like an archer – I will shoot you with the silver arrow!'

Robin thought fast.

'I don't think you will,' he said. 'Can't you hear what the people are saying? These people are my friends – you can't shoot me in front of them.'

Robin grabbed the silver arrow and blew his horn.
Will Scarlet galloped towards him on his horse, and Robin
jumped up behind him. They galloped out of the town
square. The Sheriff's men tried to follow them, but the
crowd got in their way. Robin Hood had escaped – again!

CHAPTER 9
Robin the butcher

The next day, Robin was sitting on a log in the forest. He could not forget the archery competition. He had seen Prince John pretending to be King! But where was the real King? Where was King Richard? Was he still at war, after all this time? When was he coming back? Robin had to find out …

Suddenly, he heard the sound of a horse. He jumped up from the log.

'Stop! Who goes there?' he cried.

A horse and cart came to a stop on the path in front of him.

'You must be Robin Hood!' cried the terrified man on the cart. 'Everyone in Sherwood Forest is afraid of you! Please let me go. I am just a poor butcher. I go from town to town to sell my meat. Look in my cart, and you will see that what I say is true.'

Robin looked in the cart. Meat!

'I will not hurt you,' he said to the man, 'and I will not take your money. But please do one thing for me.'

'Anything!'

'Will you lend me your horse and cart, and your meat, and your red cloak? *I* want to be a butcher!'

The man looked surprised, but he said, 'I will lend you my cart – but when can I have it back?'

'In two days' time,' said Robin. 'And I will give you any money I earn. Now, please stay here until I come back. My wife Marian will look after you.'

Robin drove the cart into Nottingham and stopped in the crowded town square.

'Best meat!' he cried. 'Come and buy my best meat, ladies!'

Then he saw the lady he was looking for – the Sheriff's wife. He smiled as he showed her a big piece of beef.

'I sell the best beef you can buy!' he told her.

The Sheriff's wife took out some money.

'I *will* buy it,' she said, 'and I will cook it for dinner tonight! Will you come and eat with us? I want my husband to meet the new butcher!'

That night, Robin sat at the Sheriff's table. He ate beef and listened to the lords and ladies.

'… and they say that the war is almost over, so King Richard will soon be back,' said one of the lords.

'Oh, no, I don't think so,' said the Sheriff. 'Prince John says that King Richard is dead. His brother, Prince John, will be our new king!'

'Not everyone thinks King Richard is dead,' said one lady.

'You are a fool! Prince John is our king now!' cried the Sheriff. He turned to Robin. 'Now tell me, butcher – where does this beef come from? It is the best we have had in this house.'

'My cows live in Sherwood Forest, sir,' said Robin. 'If you like, you can meet me there in the morning and I will show them to you. But you must come alone – cows are afraid of crowds of people.'

The next day, Robin waited in the trees for the Sheriff. He was still wearing the butcher's red cloak. When the Sheriff came, Robin said, 'Good morning, Sheriff. I will blow my horn, and the cows will come to me.'

Robin threw off his red cloak and blew his horn – but it was Merry Men, not cows, who came to him! Robin and his men took the Sheriff's money, and sent him back to Nottingham.

CHAPTER 10
The killing of Will Scarlet

One morning, Robin told Little John, 'I had a bad dream last night. I dreamed that a man in the forest caught me and made me a prisoner.'

'You worry too much, Robin!' Little John replied.

'Maybe – but I know the Sheriff and Sir Guy won't stop until they have killed us all. And then Sir Guy wants to marry my wife!' Robin said.

'But there are more Merry Men every day! Even the butcher is one of us now!' Little John replied.

'Yes, but … Come on. We'll go and see if any of the Sheriff's men are hiding in the forest. You check the river bank, and I will look in the trees.'

Little John walked along the river bank. He stopped when he saw two men. They lay, quite still, in the grass by the river, with arrows in their backs. They were dead.

'Two of our best Merry Men!' said John sadly to himself.

Suddenly, Will Scarlet ran out of the trees, followed by the Sheriff of Nottingham and three of his men.

'Will!' cried Little John, and jumped to his feet.

But it was too late. The Sheriff raised his sword and plunged it into Will's back. Will Scarlet was dead, too.

With a terrifying cry, Little John pulled out his sword. But the Sheriff and his men were too strong for him. They took his sword, and tied his hands and feet behind his back.

Robin knew nothing of this as he walked through the forest.

A man stood under a tall tree, on a carpet of red and gold leaves. Robin didn't see him at first, because he was dressed in a long hooded cloak.

The man smiled, and said, 'Maybe you can help me. I am looking for a friend of mine – Robin Hood. Do you know him?'

Robin thought fast. 'I won't tell him that *I* am Robin Hood,' he thought. 'It may be a trap.'

'Yes, I know Robin Hood,' he said. 'I will take you to him.'

When they were right in the middle of the forest, the man threw off his cloak. He was Sir Guy of Gisborn!

'I have found Robin Hood!' he cried. 'And you will die, my friend! No one can help you now!'

'You are no friend of mine – you are my enemy!' gasped Robin as he pulled out his sword.

The fight was fierce, but it was soon over. Robin plunged his sword into his enemy's heart. Sir Guy of Gisborn was dead!

Robin put on Sir Guy's cloak, and picked up Sir Guy's horn. He blew it.

Back on the river bank, the Sheriff said, 'I can hear Sir Guy's horn. I will blow mine, to tell him where we are.'

And so Robin, in his enemy's cloak, found his way to the place where the Sheriff sat on his horse with his men, and where Little John lay.

'Sir Guy!' cried the Sheriff. 'I have a prisoner for you!'

'I will kill him with one blow!' said Robin, running up to Little John.

But instead of killing his friend, he untied him!

'I am not Guy of Gisborn, Sheriff!' he laughed. 'I am your old enemy, Robin Hood! Come on, Little John – let's go!'

CHAPTER 11

The Black Knight

As Robin ran, he blew his horn. Merry Men ran up and fired arrows at the Sheriff and his men. Robin and Little John fought with their swords. They fought hard, but soon, three Merry Men were dead, and Robin was face to face with the Sheriff. The Sheriff raised his sword …

'Stop! Let that man go free!' cried a voice.

The Sheriff turned in his saddle. Behind him, Robin saw an enormous black horse. It stamped its feet and snorted like a fierce dragon. On its back sat a tall knight. He was dressed from head to foot in black armour. He wore a black cloak, and he had an enormous black sword and a black helmet.

'I am the Sheriff of Nottingham, and this man is my prisoner!' cried the Sheriff. 'Who are you?'

'You can call me the Black Knight. And do as I say, or you will be sorry!'

Something in the Black Knight's voice made the Sheriff turn his horse and ride away. His men followed him. Robin and his Merry Men were safe.

'How can I thank you, sir?' said Robin. 'Will you come back to my camp and eat dinner with us?'

'I will, Robin!' replied the knight.

'You know my name! But I don't know yours – will you tell it to me?'

The man took off his black helmet. 'I'm sorry, Robin. As you can see, I am … King Richard of England!'

Back at the camp, the King said, 'You are a good man, Robin. It is safe for you to go back to Locksley Hall now. Sir Guy is dead, and it is my wish that you have your home back. *I* must go back to war.'

The King had rescued Robin – but now that the King was away at war again, Robin knew that the Sheriff would not leave him alone for long. He kept watch night and day at Locksley Hall, with the help of Little John.

One night, as they sat at dinner, Marian said, 'This is good meat, Robin. We're lucky – the King said you can hunt as many deer as you like.'

'Yes,' said Robin. 'But we are unlucky, too – the Sheriff still wants to kill me! And I have another enemy who is even more powerful – Prince John!'

'That's true,' said Marian sadly. 'The King pardoned Prince John – but I have heard that he is making trouble again.'

'He is,' said Robin. 'Prince John says that the King is dead – and that he will rule England himself. And he says that now Sir Guy is dead, *he* will marry you – when he has killed me!'

That night, as he lay in bed, Robin heard a scraping sound on the wall of Locksley Hall. He went to find Little John. Together, they climbed onto the roof and looked down.

'It's the Sheriff!' whispered Robin. 'He's climbing up a rope to the window of my bedroom!'

Little John was angry. 'He wants to attack you while you are asleep in bed!'

'Shh!' said Robin. 'He must not hear us. I will let him climb just a little higher ...'

The Sheriff's boots scraped the wall again as he reached for the window.

Robin took his sword – and cut through the rope. With a terrible cry, the Sheriff fell to the ground – and lay still.

'Marian!' called Robin. He ran back to the bedroom. 'The Sheriff is dead! I have killed him! But our troubles are not over yet – Prince John will soon find out what I have done. He will kill me – and then he will come for you! We must leave Locksley Hall tonight! Go to your sister's house, and wait for me there!'

CHAPTER 12

Robin the sailor

When Marian had gone, Robin saddled his best horse. He rode east for three days. On the third day he saw the sea in the distance. He galloped towards it.

He came to a small village of about twenty little houses. Fishermen sat outside the houses and mended their nets.

Robin jumped off his horse and unsaddled it. He patted its nose and then sent it off into the woods – if Prince John was following him, the horse must not show his enemy where he was.

Robin walked up to one of the fishermen.

'Can you help me, sir?' he said. 'I am a fisherman, like you. But a scoundrel attacked me in the harbour, and took all my money! I have nowhere to sleep tonight!'

The man put down his net, and looked Robin up and down.

'There *are* scoundrels in our little harbour, and all good men fear them,' he said. 'Very well – come in, and I will ask my wife to make you something to eat.'

In the morning, the fisherman and his wife were talking to a sea captain.

'Soldiers on horseback are galloping all over the village!' said the captain. 'I don't know who they are looking for, but they are Prince John's men, all right. I don't like the look of them. I'm setting sail tonight.'

'Do you need another fisherman on your boat?' asked Robin. 'I am strong, and a good sailor.'

'Then I will take you on,' said the man. 'Come with me.'

The men on the boat soon found out that Robin was *not* a good sailor.

'He doesn't even know how to put up a sail!' laughed one, as he watched Robin pull at the ropes.

But Robin learned quickly. And on the third day, the sailors were pleased that he was on the boat.

'Pick up your oars! Row, as fast as you can! We're being followed by a pirate ship!' cried the captain.

Robin didn't pick up an oar – he picked up his bow and arrow. He saw that the pirate ship was moving through the water very fast. Its captain stood at the front of the ship with his sword in his hand.

Robin fitted an arrow into his bow, and raised it to his shoulder. He fired the arrow – and the pirate captain fell into the sea. Robin fired more arrows, and the other pirates soon followed their captain.

The men from Robin's boat jumped onto the pirate ship and searched it.

The captain cried out, 'Gold! Lots of gold!' He jingled some coins in his hand. 'Half of it is for you, Robin! You may not be a good sailor, but you're the best archer I've ever seen!'

CHAPTER 13

Look out, Marian!

It was very cold. The trees were white with snow. Marian pulled her cloak tightly around her as she walked. She carried the silver arrow with her, for luck.

But Marian wished Robin hadn't sent her to her sister. Marian didn't like Ann – she was greedy, and she liked money a little too much.

Smoke was rising from the chimney of Ann's little house. Marian knocked on the door.

'Come in, Marian!' said Ann. She was surprised to see her sister. 'Let me take your cloak – I will dry it for you by the fire.'

Marian kicked the snow from her shoes, and went inside.

'Sit down,' said Ann, 'and we will eat together. You can tell me all your news.'

'I need a place to hide,' said Marian as she ate. 'Robin killed the Sheriff of Nottingham. Prince John will kill him if he finds him, so he has gone away. And – Prince John wants *me* to be his wife!'

'Yes, I heard that Robin Hood had left Locksley Hall ...' said Ann thoughtfully. 'But I have heard some other news, too. People say that Robin was killed by Prince John's men.'

'Killed?' Marian's hand stopped halfway to her mouth. 'No – that can't be true! Robin is brave, and strong – he can't be dead!'

'You say that because you love him, little sister,' said Ann. She put her arm round Marian's shoulders. 'No one is safe from powerful men like Prince John. Robin is dead – and you are a rich woman! Don't forget that Robin Hood is also Sir Robin of Locksley Hall. Now that he's dead, his money is all yours! Well – yours and mine.'

Marian started to cry.

'I don't care about money! I care only for Robin!' she sobbed.

'Yes, yes,' said Ann. 'Dry your face, my dear. We must make plans. You can live with me for as long as you like. We'll be able to have everything we want, now that we have Robin's money!'

CHAPTER 14

Back to the forest

A few days later, Robin rode back from the coast and went to Ann's house.

'Ann! Are you there?' he called.

'Robin? Robin Hood?' cried Ann. She sounded angry.

'Yes, Ann, this is Robin. Is Marian here? Can I come in?'

'Marian is walking in the forest,' said Ann. 'She will be back later. Come in. Let me give you something to drink while you wait for her.'

She went to get the drink, and Robin sat down by the fire.

'Here you are!' said Ann. She put a drink in his hand. 'Drink it all – it will warm you up!'

But Robin did not drink it. Although Ann spoke kindly, there was a cruel glint in her eye, and he did not trust her. Perhaps she had put poison in the drink, so that he would die and she could have Marian all to herself!

'Now, tell me what happened after you left Locksley Hall,' said Ann.

'I went to sea in a fishing boat!' said Robin. 'And there were some pirates ... and some gold ... and the captain put me back on land ... and now I have come back for Marian!'

He sniffed the drink. It smelled bad. Now he knew that it had been poisoned! He blew his horn to call Little John.

The door opened, and Robin saw his wife.

'Robin!' cried Marian. 'I was walking in the forest and I heard your horn! You're back!' She sat down next to him. 'But you look worried! What is it, my love?'

The door opened again.

'Robin!' cried Little John. 'I've come to help you – tell me what has happened!'

'This woman … Ann … my wife's sister … she was trying to poison me, Little John! She wanted me out of the way so that Marian could come and live with her.'

Little John frowned. 'And I suppose she wanted your money as well as your wife!'

Shocked, Robin looked at Ann. 'You are a wicked woman,' he said. He took the poisoned drink and threw it at Ann. 'Here, you can have this back. But you cannot have my wife – and you cannot have my money! Come, Marian! Come, Little John! Let us go back to Sherwood Forest, where we belong!'

He flung the door open, and the three of them ran out of the house. The two men jumped onto their horses, and Robin lifted Marian up and sat her on the saddle in front of him.

Robin Hood, and his wife Marian, and his friend Little John, were soon on their way back to the forest. They were on their way home.

TEN TALL OAKTREES

Ten tall oaktrees,
Standing in a line,
'Warships,' cried King Henry,
Then there were nine.

Nine tall oaktrees,
Growing strong and straight,
'Charcoal,' breathed the furnace,
Then there were eight.

Eight tall oaktrees,
Reaching towards heaven,
'Sizzle,' spoke the lightning,
Then there were seven.

Seven tall oaktrees,
Branches, leaves and sticks,
'Firewood,' smiled the merchant,
Then there were six.

Six tall oaktrees,
Glad to be alive,
'Barrels,' boomed the brewery,
Then there were five.

Five tall oaktrees,
Suddenly a roar,
'Gangway,' screamed the west wind,
Then there were four.

Four tall oaktrees,
Sighing like the sea,
'Floorboards,' beamed the builder,
Then there were three.

Three tall oaktrees,
Groaning as trees do,
'Unsafe,' claimed the council,
Then there were two.

Two tall oaktrees,
Spreading in the sun,
'Progress,' snarled the by-pass,
Then there was one.

One tall oaktree,
Wishing it could run,
'Nuisance,' grumped the farmer,
Then there were none.

No tall oaktrees,
Search the fields in vain:
Only empty skylines
And the cold, grey rain.

Richard Edwards

LIFE IN THE DAYS OF ROBIN HOOD

The story of Robin Hood is very old. No one knows if it is true. But King Richard and Prince John were real people, and Sherwood Forest and Nottingham are real places.

Nottingham today

Sherwood Forest

What was life like for ordinary people living in England nearly 1,000 years ago, at about the time of this story?

Food

Many people were poor, and they were often hungry.
Only rich people could buy meat and cheese.
Poor people ate bread, and thick vegetable soup.
They drank water, sometimes sweetened with honey.

Clothes

People made clothes from wool.
Men and boys wore jackets
without sleeves, stockings, and
long cloaks. Women and girls
wore long skirts and tunics.
Their hair was covered by a cap.

Keeping clean

There was no gas or electricity for hot water, and it was difficult to keep clean.

School

Some boys went to school. They learned English grammar, mathematics and Latin. They sat on the floor in their classrooms.

Most girls stayed at home and learned to cook and sew.

Music and games

The people loved music and there was plenty of it –
at festivals, parties and meals. The music was made with
recorders, horns, trumpets, whistles, bells and drums.

The people also loved to watch acrobats and dancers.

They played chess and watched archery competitions.